A YEAR OF
JAPANESE FESTIVALS

A YEAR OF
JAPANESE
FESTIVALS

By Sam and Beryl Epstein

Illustrated by Gordon Laite

GARRARD PUBLISHING COMPANY
CHAMPAIGN, ILLINOIS

Library of Congress Cataloging in Publication Data

Epstein, Samuel, 1909–
    A year of Japanese festivals.

    (Around the world holidays)
    SUMMARY: Describes the celebration of several
Japanese festivals including Hi Matsuri, Girls' Day,
The One Thousand Person Procession, the Okunchi Festival,
and the Peace Festival.

        1. Festivals—Japan—Juvenile literature. [1. Fes-
tivals—Japan. 2. Japan—Social life and customs]
I. Epstein, Beryl (Williams) 1910–   joint author.
II. Laite, Gordon, illus. III. Title.
GT4884.A2E62   394.2′6952   73–22045
ISBN 0-8116-4954-7

CONTENTS

I. Let's Go to a Festival

Going to festivals is part of the way of life in Japan. And there is some kind of a festival taking place there somewhere almost every day of the year. Parents take their children to festivals. Groups of hundreds of students, on educational tours, visit a festival along the way. Club members charter buses or planes to take them to some especially popular event.

A festival is a time for dressing up. To most Japanese this means wearing their best western-style clothes. But to many little girls, and many women too, it means putting on the beautiful kimonos they save for special occasions.

A festival is also a time for taking pictures,

and almost everyone carries a camera. Some carry two or even three.

And of course a festival is a time for crowds. But even in the biggest crowd, the Japanese are usually quiet and polite. Babies, riding in cloth slings on their mothers' backs, almost never cry. Boys and girls giggle and chatter, but they seldom shout or scream. Mothers and fathers don't scold in loud voices.

Most of all, a festival is a time for having fun. There is so much to do and see!

Souvenir and food stalls line the streets leading to the spot where a festival is taking place. Often the first thing a visitor does is buy a big shopping bag. Soon it is filled with souvenirs—fans, dolls, toys, balloons, and all sorts of good-luck charms.

Smells of cooking fill the air. Some stalls are selling broiled squid, threaded on little bamboo sticks. Others sell small fried cakes, shaped like fish and filled with sweet red-bean paste.

People buy yellow ears of roasted corn and sausages dipped in batter and sizzled brown in deep fat. They buy ice cream and soda and spun-sugar candy.

Tables and benches stand in the shade beside certain stalls. Here visitors can rest and have cups of green tea or bowls of soup thick with noodles. A Japanese holds his soup bowl close beneath his chin and uses chopsticks to scoop the noodles into his mouth. The sucking, slurping noises he makes are signs of his approval.

People can also buy whole meals packed in boxes that are divided into little sections. Each section holds a different kind of food: rice, bits of pickle, slivers of radish and sharp-tasting ginger, slices of raw fish and octopus.

Children gather around the stalls that sell thin wafers with designs stamped on them. A pin comes with each wafer, and a child uses it to cut the design out by pricking around its edges. Usually the wafer breaks almost immediately. But if the design comes out whole, the child wins a small prize.

Children also like to buy chances to fish in tanks holding live eels and goldfish. The winners carry their catch away in water-filled plastic bags.

No one is in a hurry to leave the fascinating stalls. But finally everyone moves on to the festival itself. And now the real excitement begins!

2. Festivals Honor the Gods

There are many different kinds of Japanese festivals. The most common of all is the *matsuri*.

At a matsuri people may watch a splendid procession, or a contest of some kind, or a lively dance performance. They laugh and cheer and enjoy themselves. But they know, too, that they are taking part in a religious ceremony.

The word matsuri means "calling or welcoming the gods." The gods are the deities, or spirits, of Shintoism, the native Japanese religion. The Japanese name for them is *kami*.

A kami may be the spirit of the sun or of a

star, of a mountain or a field, of water or fire. Or it may be the spirit of some famous emperor or great warrior of the past. There are said to be at least eight million of these Shinto deities, and they are said to dwell in the sky or in some distant place beyond the sea.

A Japanese does not worship kami as all-powerful gods. He thinks of them, instead, as beings who are somehow superior to ordinary mortals. He believes a kami may treat him badly, and even play tricks on him. He also believes that a kami who is honored by human beings will repay those humans with help and kindness.

The most important way Japanese honor their kami is by building shrines to them. It is at these shrines that the festivals called matsuri take place.

The kami of a small valley may be honored with only one small shrine. Neighboring farmers will regard that kami as their protector, though people a few miles away may know nothing about him. The kami of a famous warrior, on the other hand, may be honored with magnificent shrines in dozens of towns all over Japan. Sometimes two or more kami are honored at a single shrine.

Every kami, it is believed, visits his own shrine

or shrines at least once a year. Each visit follows much the same pattern.

Several strong men are chosen to "meet" the kami. At the shrine they pick up a boxlike object, mounted on shafts which they carry on their shoulders. This is a portable shrine, or *mikoshi*. It may be plain, or it may be richly ornamented. It may be as small as a dollhouse or as large as a station wagon.

The young men carry the mikoshi to some place in the open—a field, perhaps, or a beach. At that place, tradition says, the kami will reach the earth after his long journey through the sky.

The young men place the mikoshi on the ground. They invite the kami to enter it. Then they carry it back and place it in the open-fronted shrine, where all may see it.

A kami's visit usually lasts three days, and during that time people try to make him feel welcome and entertain him. This entertainment is the real heart of every matsuri. If it takes the form of displays of strength and endurance, it may be dangerously wild and rough. The rougher it is, the Japanese say, the more it will be enjoyed by the kami for whom it is performed.

The Roughhouse Festival—*Kenka Matsuri*

One of the most famous of these rough festivals is the Roughhouse Festival, or *Kenka Matsuri*. It takes place in October in Shirahama, a villagelike suburb of the big city of Himeji. Its last day is the most exciting one. On that day thousands of visitors arrive from Himeji, in jam-packed trains. Others come in buses and private cars. Everybody walks the last few blocks to the festival shrine, through narrow streets lined with busy shops and souvenir stands.

As they approach the shrine, they hear the beat of drums. Many people walk straight past the stalls set up around the wall enclosing the shrine and enter through one of the wall's gates. They wish first of all to pay their respects to the visiting kami.

On the hard-packed earth inside the wall are several simple buildings. All have peaked roofs and are made of dark, unpainted wood. The smaller ones are used for storage and other purposes. The largest building is the shrine itself. A broad flight of several wooden steps leads up to its wide-open front.

All during the day, at intervals, performances

take place on the open space in front of this building. There are seven groups of performers, representing seven nearby villages or neighborhoods.

One family—father, mother, small son, and grand-mother—enters the enclosure at a moment between performances. At the little font of running water near the shrine, they rinse their hands and mouths. After this cleansing ritual they approach the foot of the shrine steps.

Above them, in the open shrine, they can see three handsome black and gold mikoshi. These portable shrines tell them that the shrine's three kami are present. The members of the family bow. They clap their hands to call the kami's attention. Then they whisper brief prayers, or appeals, and bow once more.

Each of them drops a few coins in the big wooden money box on the steps. Their offerings will help support the white-robed priests who look after the shrine and who are now standing near the mikoshi. The father hands one of the priests a brightly wrapped package of several pounds of rice, and the priest adds it to a big pile of con-tributions. Among them are evergreen branches to which strips of white paper have been tied. These

strips symbolize the cloth that was once a popular shrine offering.

Now the brief ceremony of paying respects to the kami is over. The new arrivals are ready to enjoy themselves.

A performance by one of the seven groups of entertainers is about to begin! Each of these groups has its own palanquin, a magnificent man-carried vehicle decorated in a bright color.

On the far side of the main gate the family sees a group of performers whose palanquin is decorated in green. The men are going to bring their palanquin through the gate to the open space in front of the shrine. There they will entertain the kami. Hundreds of the people inside the enclosure gather around to watch.

Suddenly the small boy notices flashes of red near the wall and points them out to his father. The color red signifies their own village. The whole family hurries over to greet their friends and admire their freshly decorated palanquin.

Like the six other festival palanquins, this one is a square wooden structure, open on all four sides. It stands some fifteen feet tall on its four stubby legs and weighs more than a thousand pounds. It can be carried by means of a pair of heavy wooden shafts which extend several yards on either side of it.

It is so fancifully decorated and carved that it looks like a miniature fairy palace. A gilded ornament tips its pointed roof. A thick silken rope—the one on this palanquin is red—loops from the roof's corners and ends in huge tassels.

Inside it, as in the other palanquins, there is barely room for a big drum and the four drummers seated around it. They wear long robes and tall hats.

One of the drummers allows the boy to climb up beside him and take his big drumstick in both hands. The boy bangs proudly on the drum. His father and mother both take his picture before he jumps down.

The twenty or so older men in the group around the palanquin are its honor guard. Their short cotton jackets are sashed tightly around their waists. The big paper pompons on the tall bamboo poles they carry are the same bright red as the palanquin's silken ropes.

The rest of the group, numbering forty or more, are the palanquin's bearers. These young men,

chosen for their skill and strength, wear only heavy canvas loincloths tied in loops at their backs. Red sweatbands hold back their straight black hair. They are joking with the admiring crowd around them. They have already performed once today and have just returned from parading their palanquin through the neighboring streets. They are resting now, while the green-decorated palanquin appears before the shrine.

Suddenly their leader gives a signal. The green-decorated palanquin is being carried toward a corner of the enclosure. The red palanquin's moment has come!

The honor guards lift their pompons high. The bearers line up, one man close behind the other, along the heavy shafts. The drummers strike up a slow steady beat.

The little boy looks up at the high wooden platform mounted on top of the wall near the main gate. The television and press photographers there have shifted their cameras toward the red palanquin. The boy hopes his picture will be in the paper the next day, or perhaps on television that same night.

The leader gives another signal. The bearers

stoop down, put their shoulders beneath the palanquin's shafts, and heave it off the ground. Then, to the beat of the drum, and surrounded by the honor guard, they trot toward the front of the shrine. The boy and his family follow, squeezing through the crowd to reach a good place for watching the performance.

In front of the shrine the palanquin bearers halt for a moment, and the honor guard moves away to give them plenty of room. Then, as the drums go on beating, they carry their burden to the right, to the left, forward and back, around and around.

The drum beats quicken. The heavy palanquin spins faster and faster. The men are almost running.

Suddenly the great palanquin plunges straight toward one section of the watching crowd. The nearest spectators scream and back hastily out of the way. At the last possible moment the bearers halt, and again the palanquin revolves in front of the shrine.

The leader issues another command. This time the young men lift the great shafts off their shoulders. The palanquin rises in the air until it is held at arms' length over the men's heads. All around it the honor guard's pompons form a tossing red sea.

Then the bearers, at a word from their leader, let go of their burden. The palanquin drops with an earth-shaking crash. The drummers bounce high against the roof. The ribbons on their tall hats whip back and forth. But they never miss a beat.

Over and over the bearers lift the palanquin high—and drop it. Over and over the drummers bounce against the roof without losing their rhythm.

Finally the palanquin is thrust high once more, but this time it is not dropped. Instead the bearers let it tip to one side, as if they had lost control over it. It tilts so far over that the watchers gasp in alarm. One drummer is almost flat on his back now. The man opposite him hangs face down in his seat, and the other two lie sideways. Still all four of them go on drumming.

Slowly, aided by the poles of the honor guard, the palanquin comes upright again. The crowd cheers. Then, while the drumming goes on and sweat pours down the bearers' backs, the whole performance is repeated. The red palanquin group hopes to outdo all the others, and thus win the kami's approval.

Finally, at the end of twenty minutes or so, the group retires. It will rest briefly while men with a blue-decorated palanquin prepare to take its place and put on a similar show. Then the red group will again parade its palanquin through the town. The little boy will want to follow them, but his parents will insist that they remain to watch the next performance.

The Roughhouse Festival lives up to its name. Its final hours are the roughest of all. They begin when the entertainment is over and the kami are said to be ready to depart for their spirit home.

Each kami's portable shrine, or mikoshi, is entrusted to a group of strong young men. Other men with long bamboo poles surround them. All three mikoshi are carried down to the open space before the shrine.

Immediately, one group of bearers dash themselves and their mikoshi against another group. The bearers of the second mikoshi push back. Onlookers take sides, shouting insults and encouragement.

Suddenly a young man climbs to the roof of one mikoshi and tugs at the gilded bird on its top. The mikoshi's protectors slash at his legs with their

poles. The bearers rock the mikoshi back and forth, trying to topple the young man from his perch.

Somehow he hangs on until the gold figure comes off in his hands. He hurls it into the crowd with a triumphant shout and leaps after it.

Two by two, and sometimes all three at once, the mikoshi battle each other. All finally lose their gilded birds. All become heavily scarred.

At last a truce is called. A procession forms around the mikoshi and moves out through the gate. In the procession are floats filled with boy pipers and drummers. Town officials in kimonos and Shinto priests in white robes join the line of march. Around them all surges the festival crowd.

The slow parade ends at a field between two steep hills. The slopes of both hills are packed solid with thousands of spectators.

Before this huge audience the battered mikoshi fight their last fight. It goes on, to the shouts of the crowd, until the festival's officials order a halt.

The day ends quietly. A brief ritual bids farewell to the kami. The mikoshi—or what is left of them—are returned to the shrine. There they will be repaired and stored until next year. Weary bearers take their palanquins back to their own

24

communities. These too will have to be repaired and made ready to appear again.

Slowly the crowd drifts away, toward cars and buses and the local railroad station. Proprietors of food and souvenir stalls take down their flimsy little booths and load them into trucks. Soon they are on their way to another town, where they will set up their stalls in time for its matsuri.

The Roughhouse Festival has ended. The gods, everyone hopes, have been well pleased.

Fire Festival—*Hi Matsuri*

Men and boys also show off their strength at the Fire Festival, or *Hi Matsuri*, in the mountain village of Kurama.

Early on an October evening, bonfires are lit along Kurama's single street, which slopes sharply uphill to the stairs leading to a shrine. Local families and their guests are already looking down from second-floor windows. Hundreds of visitors are jammed between the shop fronts and the narrow roped-off passageway along the middle of the street. Trainloads of new arrivals pour out of the village railroad station every few minutes to join the throng.

Suddenly a wave of laughter sweeps through the village. Walking up the hill, in the center of the roped-off passage, comes a very small boy in a kimono. He is carrying a little torch made of flaming twigs. His mother is beside him, guiding him and helping him hold his torch. He is the first of the torchbearers who will parade up and down this street for hours.

Other small children follow, one by one. Next come older boys carrying larger torches. They chant rhythmically as they walk. "*Sai-rei! Sai-ryo! Sai-rei! Sai-ryo!*" Onlookers pick up the meaningless words and shout them back.

Young men in loincloths and short cotton coats follow the boys. They carry three-foot torches of sticks and branches, burning in cone-shaped baskets made of green bamboo slats. Then come the adults, with torches that weigh several hundred pounds. Two or three men share the weight of one of these great flaming cones.

As the night wears on, the younger torchbearers are taken home to bed. The older ones grow tipsy. They have drunk many glasses of *sake*, a Japanese rice wine, as they rested between journeys up and down the street.

Now and then a torch-bearing team staggers toward one side of the passage. People behind the ropes press backward, out of the way. Sparks fly wildly. Sometimes a heavy torch is dropped, and bits of burning wood scatter on every side.

But there is no panic. Fire is a purifying force according to Shinto belief. It protects against evil spirits. So no one is really frightened by the flying sparks. Many people even try to catch one, because they believe it will bring them luck.

By midnight the torches are burned out, and the torch-bearing comes to an end. A hush falls over the village. Spectators and torchbearers together line up on both sides of the long flight of steps leading to the shrine.

At the head of the steps a Shinto priest cuts the rope that has been tied across the shrine entrance. Two teams of sturdy young men, about forty in each team, pick up two brilliantly decorated mikoshi. Carefully they carry their heavy burdens down the stairs.

A silent crowd follows them along the street, past the smoldering bonfires. At an open area at the edge of town, the mikoshi are set down. Priests murmur a farewell ritual. The kami depart.

Bonten Festival

A year of good luck is said to be the reward of the winning team at the Bonten Festival in Akita. This festival takes place in February, when this northern region is covered with ice and snow.

Each team of young men represents a district of the city. Each has its own *bonten*. This is a ten-foot bamboo pole, draped with heavy cloth and topped by a circular platform. On the platform is a figure of the Animal of the Year. Every year is named for an animal according to the old oriental calendar. Twelve animal names are used, one for each year in the calendar's twelve-year cycles. Each cycle begins with a Year of the Rat and continues through the Years of the Ox, Tiger, Rabbit, Dragon, Snake, Horse, Sheep, Monkey, Cock, Dog, and Boar. In a Year of the Rabbit, therefore, the figures on all the bonten are rabbits.

On the day of the festival, the teams stage a race through the city to the shrine whose kami they are honoring. Members of each team, perhaps two or three men at a time, take turns carrying its bonten. It is a long race. They start off at a walk.

A bonten is heavy. Its long draperies catch the

wind. The bearers do their best to keep it up-right, and walk quickly. The race is not easy. But the bearers manage to increase their pace as they go.

The final stretch of the way to the shrine is a steep hill. The contestants are running by the time they reach it. Spectators are cheering them on.

On the icy slope the men fight for footing. They also fight each other, as each team tries to delay the rest. A team that has almost reached the top may be knocked off its feet, to slide helplessly back to the bottom of the hill.

Finally one team reaches the shrine and wins the honor of presenting its bonten to the kami. After placing the heavy object inside the shrine, the young men are guests of honor at a party. Their friends agree they deserve a real celebration.

3. Festivals Are History

Japan today is one of the most modern nations in the world.

One reason is that, during the twentieth century, some of her cities were flattened by earthquakes or other disasters, and then completely rebuilt. Among them is Tokyo, capital of Japan since 1868. Tokyo was built anew after it had been destroyed by fire bombs during World War II.

Another reason why Japan is so modern is that the country has been rapidly industrialized since 1853. That year she opened her doors to western influence after centuries of isolation from the rest of the world. Before that date she had been an agricultural nation. Since then she has become

one of the world's most efficient producers of manu-
factured goods.

But modern Japan preserves and cherishes many
links with the earliest days of her long and colorful
history. Among them, for example, are many
shrines built hundreds of years ago. And in the
very heart of Tokyo, hidden behind moats and high
stone walls, stands Japan's Imperial Palace. Legend
says that the emperor dwelling there today is
descended from the gods who created the Japanese
islands in the dim and distant past.

But probably the past comes most vividly alive
for the Japanese when they attend some festival
that has been celebrated year after year for centuries. One of these is the *Gion Matsuri* of Kyoto.

Gion Festival

Kyoto, often called "the real heart of old Japan,"
was the seat of the imperial court for 1,100 years.
During that period its magnificent annual processions had their beginnings. The Gion Matsuri,
which takes place in July, dates from the year 869.

That year the city was ravaged by an epidemic,
and the emperor sought help from one of his god-
ancestors. His appeal took the form of a display

set up before the Gion Shrine, dedicated to that ancestor. It consisted of 66 long-handled spears, or halberds, one for each of the emperor's provinces.

Shortly afterward the city was freed of disease, and the emperor expressed his gratitude with a grand procession. The floats prepared for it were called *hoko*, or halberd, and *yama*, or mountain. Today's procession still consists of these two kinds of floats. Some of them are centuries old.

A hoko is a towerlike box on wheels which weighs as much as ten tons. It is topped by a long pole representing a halberd. The smaller yama, weighing perhaps a ton, is a platform mounted on carrying shafts. On it is placed a "mountain" of objects—models of human and animal figures, and sacred relics from the shrine. After each festival the floats are taken apart and stored away.

The work of putting them together again begins about ten days before the festival. The group of men responsible for each one does its work on a street corner, and townspeople gather around to watch.

The men in each hoko-assembling group first fasten heavy timbers together, with rice-straw ropes, to form a platform. At each of its corners

is a wooden wheel some eight feet across. On the platform they erect a roofed tower and drape it with scarlet cloth. Usually they have to set up scaffolds, or build a bridge out from a nearby second-story window, in order to complete their job. Finally they place on the hoko's roof its halberd-shaped pole, which may be forty feet high.

The ornament on the pole's tip gives each float its name. The one tipped by a crescent moon, for example, is called the Tsuki Hoko, or Moon Halberd.

The smaller yama are being put together at the same time. Each has its own name and decorations. One, called the Float of the Carp, is dedicated to the festival deity. The figures on its platform illustrate an ancient legend about a carp that was changed into a dragon.

In the meantime a young boy has been named the festival's page boy. While the floats are being put together, he travels around the city and watches the work in progress. An attendant waves a huge fan over him wherever he goes. The boy's face is painted white, and he wears the flowing white robe and peaked hat of a Shinto priest. His parents and brothers and sisters, also in costume, travel with him and share in the excitement.

On the night before the procession, paper lanterns are strung on all the floats and lighted. Bands of musicians then take their places in each hoko. There are flutists and drummers and men who strike big gongs with metal-tipped sticks. They start to play immediately. They will continue to play until the procession is over the next day. Strips of brocade, hanging from the drummers' sticks, rise and fall in time to their beat.

At the same time the lanterns, set up along the streets by Kyoto's shopkeepers, are lighted. And some of Kyoto's aristocratic old families open their homes to the public and permit people to view their most precious heirlooms.

Kyoto residents, and the thousands of visitors who have come to the city for this festival, stroll about in the lantern glow. They listen to the musicians. At the lighted doorways of the open homes, they remove their shoes, as the Japanese always do before stepping on the soft straw mats that carpet their floors. Then they bow and step inside to admire jade carvings, decorated silk scrolls, and the swords of feudal war lords.

The day of the procession dawns. City workmen are the first to travel along the parade route.

Their job is to take down any electric wires that might catch in the tall poles of the hoko. Later in the day the workmen will restore the wires.

By early morning men are busy adding the final decorations to all the floats. They hang lengths of the richly colored silks for which Kyoto has always been famous. They use valuable tapestries too. These were given to the Gion Matsuri years ago by wealthy Kyoto merchants who imported them from Europe.

Soon young men wearing short cotton coats and pointed straw hats gather around each float. They are its "crew." With them are older men, dressed in ancient court costumes, who will walk ahead of the float. The crew of a yama will carry its float by its shafts. The crew of a hoko will pull its heavy float by means of long ropes.

Now, at each hoko, other men take their appointed places. Four of them climb to the roof, where each clings to one corner. The big sleeves of their kimonos are bulging with *chimaki*, handfuls of straw wrapped in bamboo leaves. During the procession they will toss them into the crowd, and people will scramble wildly to catch these good-luck charms.

Two other men, with scarlet and white fans, also climb aboard. Their station is the hoko's narrow front platform. To keep their footing they must hang on to a rope fastened to the roof. During the procession they will wave their fans to urge on the hoko crew.

Finally all is ready. Priests purify the hoko by sprinkling salt over its wheels. The small page boy takes his place of honor in the hoko that will lead the procession. Fifty or more men line up along its ropes.

A signal is given. The men pull on the ropes and strain to set the big awkward vehicle in motion. Slowly the hoko moves away from its corner and heads down the street to the music of the tireless musicians. The procession has started.

Gradually, one by one, the other floats move in from their own assembly stations and form a line behind the leader. Usually there are about twenty of them.

The heavy wheels of the hoko grind noisily along the pavement at a dignified snail's pace. Those wheels are not made to be steered. Each time the procession turns a corner, every hoko must be shoved and tugged around with great effort. Men

and boys in the crowd lining the route often run out to grab the ropes and help.

Most of the city's businesses have been closed for the day. Everyone seems to be out in the streets. Every float is cheered and applauded. Each one seems more spectacular than the last. This great procession is a sight no Japanese ever forgets.

The procession ends with each float back at its starting place. There it will be carefully taken apart so that it can be stored away until next year's Gion Matsuri.

The One Thousand Person Procession

The little town of Nikko lies high in the mountains in one of Japan's great national parks. Its splendid shrines and temples, and its avenues bordered with towering trees, are famous all over Japan. A popular saying is, "Never say kekko until you have seen Nikko." The word *kekko* means "magnificent."

Nikko's One Thousand Person Procession illustrates the grandeur of Japan's feudal period. That period began in the twelfth century and lasted for several hundred years. During all that time the emperor was shut away in his palace, almost a prisoner. The ruling power was held by first one, then another, of Japan's great clans, or families. A clan leader controlled both the emperor and his people. He was called the *shogun*, or military dictator. He maintained his authority through his army of faithful warriors known as *samurai.*

After the death of one powerful shogun, in 1616, his grandson decided to build a mausoleum and shrine in his honor. From all over Japan he summoned the finest craftsmen to Nikko. From every vassal war lord he demanded contributions. The finished buildings were splendid with carvings, brilliant lacquers, and sheets of gold. Enough gold was used, it was said, to cover five acres of ground. The procession that carried the shogun's remains to the mausoleum is now repeated every May.

Shinto priests, some on horseback, some carrying brightly colored banners, head the long line of march. Behind them come hundreds of men dressed as warriors of the seventeenth and eighteenth centuries. They wear helmets of fantastic shapes, some topped with deer antlers. Their tunics and big square shoulder guards are made of metal strips, held together by cords or leather thongs.

Most of the soldiers carry bows and arrows or

long spears, but one troop bears old matchlock guns. These weapons were introduced to Japan in the sixteenth century by Portuguese traders, the first Europeans to enter Japanese ports.

The heads of some marchers are covered with shaggy manes. They represent lions, who are said to protect roads from evil. Other men wear fox masks and represent the fox spirits said to dwell in the mountains around Nikko.

And of course there are the drummers and other musicians who accompany all Japanese processions.

The day ends with a remarkable contest called *yabusame*. Yabusame, or archery on horseback, was a favorite sport of the samurai warriors.

The contest takes place on a fenced-off course about ninety yards long. At regular intervals, on each side of the course, small square targets are attached to the fence. There are six of them altogether. The bowmen, mounted on specially trained horses, wear wide-brimmed hats and kimonos with flowing sleeves. They carry their arrows in big quivers on their backs.

Each rider sets off alone down the course, riding at full gallop. Drawing and aiming with great speed, he tries to hit each of the three targets on the fence to his left. Then he pivots at the end of the course and rides back, aiming for the other three targets as he goes. A bowman skillful enough to hit all six targets wins an enthusiastic round of applause.

The *Okunchi* Festival in Nagasaki

Nagasaki, Japan's westernmost port, has its own share of history and its own historic festivals. Its famous *Okunchi* Festival pays tribute to the Chinese and Dutch traders whose ships anchored here long ago.

Chinese traders first came to Japan in the earliest days of her history. They helped introduce China's advanced civilization to Japan. It was from China, for example, that the Japanese learned the art of writing.

The first Dutch traders, on the other hand, did not arrive until the sixteenth century, after Portuguese seamen had shown them the way. For about a century they carried on a lively trade with Japan. Then the ruling shogun barred foreigners from all ports except Nagasaki. That harbor alone was permitted to receive a few Dutch and Chinese ships every year. Until Japan once more opened her ports to foreigners, in the 1850s, those ships were her link with the outside world.

In their honor, a Dutch dance and a Chinese dragon dance are performed at the Okunchi Festival. The dances take place in the open space, or arena, at the foot of the long flight of steps leading to a Shinto shrine. Priests and city officials watch from those steps. Other spectators kneel in Japanese fashion on the sloping platforms set up on either side.

Each family, or group of three or four friends, occupies its own "box" on those platforms. This is a section of straw matting, about a yard square, marked off by bamboo poles. Somehow, even in such crowded quarters, most of them find room for parcels of food, toys for the children, and several cameras. The shoes which everyone removed before stepping on the matting have been put in plastic bags, and these too are tucked away somewhere in the box.

The Dutch dance is performed by two girls, one taking the part of a man. Both wear the costumes worn by early Dutch visitors to the city. The false mustache of the "man" amuses the crowd on sight. And the audience continues to laugh as the dancers flirt with each other, bow, smirk, and prance about.

During the intermission after the Dutch dance, people in the stands eat some of the food they have brought along. They drink tea from thermos jugs, or open cans or bottles of beer and soda. Cameras click busily. But everyone watches the corner of the arena for the first glimpse of the snakelike Chinese "dragons."

Suddenly there is a hush. The four dragons appear. They are made of cloth, stretched over flexible frames, and have huge dragon heads. Two are about fifty feet long, with bodies as large around as a man's. The other two are smaller.

Each dragon has its own team of about a dozen dancers, wearing round black caps, short white jackets, and tight black trousers. Each dancer helps carry the dragon by holding one of the many black rods attached to its body. Men carry the two large dragons. Young boys carry the other two.

Each dragon gives a solo performance. Its bearers, stepping in time to drum beats, shift their carrying rods from hand to hand and raise and lower their arms. These motions make the dragon "dance." The long body rises and falls with snakelike motions.

It twists from side to side. It tosses its huge head and twitches its long tail. And it constantly "attacks" a man who carries a long pole topped by a golden globe.

The globe represents the sun. The dragon, representing darkness, is said to be trying to destroy the light of the world. At the end of each dance, the globe is lifted high in the air, and the dragon bows its head in defeat. The sun always wins this legendary battle.

Other performers entertain at the Okunchi Festival too. There are musicians, for example. And there are groups of young men who push big wooden floats into the arena and race them about at breakneck speed.

But the Okunchi Festival is a matsuri, and thus it follows the traditional matsuri pattern. It begins with the mikoshi being taken from the shrine to fetch the visiting kami. It ends when the empty mikoshi are brought back to the shrine after the kami's departure. And the return of the mikoshi forms an exciting climax to this particular festival. Even spectators exhausted by three days of performances, feasting, and souvenir-buying join the crowd along the narrow street leading up to the shrine. That street is so steep that in some places it takes the form of steps.

The sound of drums signals the approach of the mikoshi procession. White-robed Shinto priests appear first, some carrying money boxes into which people toss small paper-wrapped coins. Then come important citizens of the town, wearing black kimonos and carrying fans. The drums accompanying the marchers are so huge that each is slung from a long wooden pole carried by two young priests. Other priests, walking alongside, bang the drums with slow rhythmic strokes.

Finally the brightly lacquered and gilded mikoshi come in sight. Each rests on two long shafts born on the shoulders of a dozen young men. The bearers are breathing hard, but they move faster as they near the top of the hill. They break into a run when they approach the arena before the steep flight of steps leading to the shrine.

Then, with a final burst of energy, they dash across the arena and run up the whole long flight without a single pause. They reach the top exhausted but full of pride. They have proved that they deserved the honor of serving as mikoshi-bearers. Many of them began dreaming of that honor when they were small boys, watching their first Okunchi Festival.

Peace Festival

One important twentieth-century event in Japan's history is now commemorated by its own festival. That event took place on August 6, 1945. On that day an American plane dropped an atomic bomb on the city of Hiroshima and totally destroyed it. The terrible effects of that first atomic attack helped bring about Japan's surrender and the end of World War II.

Now every year, on August 6, the rebuilt city of Hiroshima holds a Peace Festival. It takes place at the monument honoring the thousands of bomb victims. There is no gaiety in this festival. It is a solemn occasion. And it looks ahead, rather than back to the past. On this day the people of Japan pledge themselves to a future of peace for their own nation and for the world.

49

4. Festivals Honor People

Some of the most important national festivals in Japan honor people rather than gods. There are festivals in honor of the old people and the young people. There are boys' festivals and girls' festivals. There are festivals in honor of people who have recently died.

Boys' Festival

In late April and early May, brightly colored paper or cloth carp, a kind of fish, flutter from poles all over Japan. Some poles rise from the tiny yards that front most Japanese houses. Some are set up on rooftops. In one way or another,

most Japanese families fly fish-shaped streamers every spring.

The Japanese say that the carp has strength, courage, and determination. These are qualities they hope their sons will acquire. So this fish has long been the symbol of Boys' Festival, which takes place on the fifth of May.

Sons are very important in Japan. A man must have sons, the Japanese say, to fulfill family obligations, to carry on the family name, and to honor a father's memory after his death.

As Boys' Festival approaches, a Japanese family buys a paper or cloth carp for each of its sons. The largest fish—it may be more than fifteen feet long—is for the eldest son. It is given the highest position, just under the pinwheel which adorns the top of each pole. Below it goes a smaller fish for the next younger brother, and so on down the pole until all the carp are in place. Even a newborn baby boy has his own very small carp in the lowest position on the pole.

If a family has several sons, its pole is a spectacular and colorful sight. Each time the wind blows, the carp puff up and dart back and forth as if they were alive.

The other traditional preparations for the festival take place inside the house. There parents arrange shelves on which they place miniature helmets, suits of armor, swords, spears, and bows and arrows. Among them may also be small figures dressed as samurai warriors. All these objects are said to inspire the young boys to be brave, strong, and determined.

On the morning of the festival, the members of a Japanese family traditionally take a special kind of bath called *shobu-ya*. In the Shinto belief, water is a great purifier. It can wash away bad spirits and bad luck. To the Japanese, therefore, a bath does more than cleanse the body.

Japanese soap, scrub, and rinse themselves before getting into their deep tubs. The hot tub water is to soak in, to relax tired muscles and nerves. After the father finishes soaking, the mother and children follow him, one at a time, into the still-clean water.

Usually the Japanese bathe late in the day so that they are refreshed for their evening meal. On this festival, however, the family bathes early, and its tub water is scented with the sword-shaped iris leaves called *shobu*. Samurai warriors once used shobu in their tubs, and the Japanese say the leaves give strength and vigor.

Today many Japanese feel their sons should no longer be encouraged to model themselves on samurai warriors and other military heroes. The government has therefore established a new national holiday called Children's Day. It honors boys and girls alike and encourages them to love and respect each other. Its date is the same as that of Boys' Festival.

Many young children are taken to Shinto shrines on this day. Those old enough to walk are led to stand in front of it. Babies are carried there by parents or grandparents. The tall shrine flagpoles are decorated with silk carp—black-speckled ones for boys, reddish-colored ones for girls. A priest waves a wand of white paper streamers over the children and then faces the shrine to ask for their happiness and health.

Afterward everyone returns home for a special meal. Most mothers have prepared their children's favorite sweets. Then, whether a family is celebrating Boys' Festival or Children's Day, or both together, there is a great deal of visiting back and forth among neighbors, relatives, and friends.

Girls' Day

As March comes around there is an air of excitement in most Japanese households. Little girls giggle more than usual. They can hardly wait for their older sisters and parents to open certain boxes which have been stored away for a year.

Inside the boxes are special dolls called *hina*, which means "something small and lovely." The dolls are the most important feature of the *Hina Matsuri*, or Doll Festival, usually called Girls' Day. It takes place on March 3 and is as important to girls as Boys' Festival is to boys.

Long ago this was a Shinto spring-welcoming ritual. Its purpose was to cleanse away winter's evil spirits. People rubbed themselves with small paper dolls, in the belief that any evil spirits within their own bodies would leave them and enter the dolls. Then they threw the dolls into a stream, to be purified and carried away. Because peach trees bloomed at the time the ritual was performed, it was sometimes called the Peach Blossom Festival.

As time went by people began to use clay dolls instead of paper ones. Craftsmen began to make such pretty dolls that people did not want to

throw them away, so they set them on shelves to be admired.

About two hundred years ago skilled craftsmen began to model their dolls after ancient Japanese royalty. Two tiny figures were dressed like a Japanese emperor and his wife. Others were dressed like court attendants and servants. There were also miniature dogs, palace furniture, and orange trees for a royal garden.

These tiny figures became carefully guarded family treasures. Wealthy parents bought a complete set for a daughter as soon as she was born. Poor people saved to buy at least a few dolls for their girl babies. When girls grew up and married, they kept their doll displays for their own daughters.

A traditional set of fifteen dolls, along with furniture, trees, and other objects, is displayed on a rack of seven shelves covered with red cloth. A branch of flowering peach is usually placed near the shelves.

There is a great deal of visiting on Girls' Day. Guests come to see a family's display and to enjoy special foods the hostess has prepared. The little girls are often told that this is a lucky day for weddings, and many of them grow up wanting to be married on March 3.

Shichi-Go-San

Japanese believe that certain ages are so unlucky that all who survive them owe special thanks to the gods. That is the reason for the children's holiday called *Shichi-Go-San*, which occurs on November 15. Its name means "seven-five-three." It is a holiday for girls aged seven and three, and for boys aged five and three.

Shichi-Go-San usually begins with a grateful family's visit to a shrine. The children are dressed in their best clothes. Many little girls wear brightly-colored kimonos with big butterfly-shaped bows on their backs. Many boys wear kimonos too, often bought especially for this day. Each child carries a paper bag decorated with good-luck signs.

After the family has paid its respects at the shrine, the fun of filling the paper bags begins. Priests give the children candy. Their parents buy them toys and souvenirs from the stalls set up near the shrine. By the time a family is ready to go home, each child's bag is filled.

Then, at home, a child may receive more presents from visiting friends and relatives. And the day often ends with a party to celebrate the happy occasion.

Bon Festival

On the Festival of *Bon,* or *Obon,* as it is sometimes called, the Japanese joyfully welcome the spirits of their dead. These spirits are said to return to their earthly home for a three-day visit each summer.

Bon is a Buddhist festival. It has been celebrated ever since the Buddhist religion was brought to Japan from India, by way of China, fourteen centuries ago. Millions of Japanese are Buddhists as well as Shintoists. The Buddhism practiced in Japan does not interfere with the people's older Shinto religion.

A person may go to a Shinto shrine to ask a kami's help toward a good harvest. Then that person may go to a Buddhist temple, the same day, for a very different reason. There he is not asking for a good harvest, or for anything that would make life easier or more pleasant. Instead he is praying for help in learning the self-discipline taught by Buddha, the religion's great teacher. Buddhism promises a new and better life after death for those who have earned it by self-discipline on earth.

In most of Japan, Bon takes place on July 13, 14, and 15. It comes a month later in rural areas, where people still use the lunar calendar. By that calendar the year begins with the full moon of February. Whatever the date, families clean their homes from top to bottom, to prepare them for their spirit visitors. They make sure their family graves are neat and tidy. At special Bon markets they buy evergreen branches, flowers, incense, fruits, and vegetables. Often they buy crickets in tiny cages to make their homes cheerful.

On the day the festival begins, each family lays a special mat before the Buddhist altar in its home. On this altar, which may be only a small table, are tiny tablets that honor each family member who has recently died. The tablets look rather like miniature gravestones. Usually a small statue of a Buddha stands among them. On the mat are placed offerings of flowers, fruits, or vegetables, and portions of the foods the spirits were fond of when they were alive.

Then the family goes to the cemetery, which is often beside a Buddhist temple. They decorate each grave with green branches, and light incense at the foot of its stone marker. On the grave they place rice cakes and other offerings to welcome the spirits.

They are home again before dark to light a small fire outside their house or set a white paper lantern just outside their door.

At last all is ready. When darkness falls they light more white lanterns and carry them to the graveyard. The smell of incense now fills the air, and the night is lighted by softly glowing lanterns. Many family groups have come, and at each freshly decorated grave they solemnly invite their ancestral spirits to join them.

From that moment on, for the next two days, the living members of the family behave as if their ancestors were with them. They guide the spirits home by lantern light and remind them to avoid rough spots in the road. When they reach their doorway, with its welcoming light, they urge their guests to enter and enjoy the meal set out for them.

Then the living members of the family enjoy a

feast of their own. Often they invite a Buddhist priest to share it, and before leaving he chants some of the Buddhist scriptures.

When evening comes on the third day, the members of the family serve rice dumplings for the spirits' last meal. Again they light a fire or set out a lantern at their door. Then, with respectful bows, they bid the spirits farewell.

People who live near a body of water usually invite the departing spirits to embark in a small toy boat made of straw or wood. They place a lighted candle or miniature paper lantern in its bow and a small dish of burning incense in its stern. Then they set the tiny craft adrift and watch it float away into the dark.

The young people of some communities celebrate the last night of Bon with a *Bon-Odori*, or Bon dance. They practice long hours for the event and appear in specially made hats and kimonos. There may be hundreds of young people dancing at the same time, in pairs or in small groups. They twirl to the beat of drums, spinning faster and faster, stamping their feet, and clapping their hands. They stop suddenly, and all hold the same motionless pose until the twirling starts again. As soon as

they finish one dance, they start another to a different rhythm. A Bon-Odori may go on until dawn, while most of the community looks on.

The city of Kyoto ends its Bon festival with a dramatic fire on the slope of a nearby hill. On that slope are dozens of concrete boxes set out in rows to form a design. It looks rather like a letter A more than 400 feet tall. This is the Japanese character pronounced *dai*, which means "big."

For weeks before the festival, volunteers are busy cleaning out the grass that has grown in and around the boxes. Then they lay a fire in each one. On the night of August 16 the fires are lit all at once.

Swiftly the flames spread and join, forming a great fiery pattern against the dark hillside. The blazing dai can be seen for miles around. Nowhere in Japan do the spirits have a more magnificent light to guide them on their way back to their heavenly home.

5. Festivals of the Seasons

All Japanese, even city dwellers, feel a strong closeness to nature. This feeling is expressed in festivals for the snows of winter, the flowers of spring, summer, and early fall, and the blazing colors of late autumn foliage.

The Sapporo Snow Festival

On the first Thursday of February, every year, the main square of the city of Sapporo is a winter fairyland created out of snow and ice. In this vast open space stand shining white copies of famous statues and figures of famous people. There are huge ice castles, some over sixty feet high. In one corner crowds can admire the snow model of an ancient Greek temple. In another they gape at a snowy white rocket spaceship. Thousands of people wander through the large square on that opening night of Sapporo's Snow Festival. Hundreds of thousands more will come to see the display during the next three days and nights. This is one of the most famous festivals in Japan, even though it was not started until the year 1950.

Sapporo, on the island of Hokkaido, is the northernmost big city of Japan. It is usually blanketed by snow for months every year. By November crews are out cleaning its streets, and trucks are hauling tons of snow to dumping areas. About the middle of January, however, those trucks start carrying their loads to the city's main square. They are delivering the 14,000 tons of snow that will be needed for the sculpture display. At the same time big blocks of ice are cut from the frozen river nearby, and these too are hauled to the square.

Finally the 2,000 workers the city has hired appear in the square and are divided into teams. Each team is assigned to its own project and its own space.

Some teams work with nothing but snow. They build up a big mound of it, packing it hard as the mound grows. Then they chop away at the packed snow, as if it were a block of marble. Slowly a figure begins to take shape.

Other teams first build a steel frame. One team, for example, may build the frame of a big steam locomotive. Then the workers pack snow around the frame, covering every part of it with great care. The result is a gleaming locomotive, perfectly snow-white to its last nut and bolt.

Still other teams are stacking up many layers of ice blocks, pouring water over each layer as it is added. The water freezes, holding all the blocks together in one solid shining pile. Then these workers too begin chopping away, as if the ice were marble. The finished figure is as transparent as glass.

At the end of two weeks, all is ready for the great opening night of the festival. There are parades and ice-skating and skiing contests. But what brings so many people here each year are the shapes of snow and ice that glisten in the sun and sparkle under blazing lights at night.

A week or two after the festival ends, big bulldozers flatten the sculptures, and trucks cart away the crumbled snow and shattered ice. Traffic again moves through the great open square that is the

heart of busy Sapporo. But already the people are thinking about next year's festival. Everyone is determined that it will be even bigger and more beautiful than the last.

Kamakura Festival

Winter throws a thick covering of snow over the northern corner of Japan's main island of Honshu. There, in the town of Yokote, children build round snow huts for a February festival called *Kamakura*. The huts are generally made by hollowing out a big snow drift. They look like little igloos.

Usually all the children of one family work together to make a hut. When it is finished, they light it with candles or with an electric light. They smooth out the snow floor and cover it with a thick straw mat. They set a small shelf against the wall to serve as a Shinto shrine to the god of water. On it they put lighted candles and offerings such as rice cakes, fruit, and rice wine. They start a fire in a *hibachi*, or charcoal stove.

Each child has left his shoes outside. But everyone wears warm socks and slippers and is wrapped in a thick quilt called a *futon*.

The children heat sweet wine and sip it from

small cups. They eat rice cakes they have toasted over the fire.

One of the things the children enjoy most is receiving visitors. Parents and neighbors stop in front of the doorway and bow. The children invite them to enter. The visitors remove their shoes and bend down to step into the little hut. The children make them comfortable around the fire and serve wine and rice cakes. Usually the visitors leave a gift of fruit or a few coins for their young hosts when they depart. Some children are even allowed to spend the night in their Kamakura houses.

Setsubun

The beginning of the end of winter is celebrated all over Japan with an unusual bean-throwing festival. It is called *Setsubun,* which means "season change." Its purpose is to drive away evil spirits before the coming of spring.

House doorways are decorated with tree branches and heads of sardines. The prickly leaves on the branches are said to poke out demons' eyes. The smell of the sardines is said to drive demons away.

The bean-throwing ceremony begins after sunset, on the evening of February 3. The head of the house takes handfuls of dried beans from a wooden box and throws them into each room, even into each closet. As the other members of the family follow behind, they shout, *"Oni wa soto!"* ("Out with the devils!") Then the head of the house stands in each room and closet in turn and throws beans outward. This time the others shout, *"Fuku wa uchi!"* ("Come in, good spirits!")

Some families prefer to attend a public Setsubun ceremony, before a Shinto shrine or a Buddhist temple. There several important men appear on a balcony early in the evening.

At a given signal these "year men," as they are called, throw beans into the crowd. Everyone tries to catch some, because tradition says these beans bring good luck.

In Nara, not far from Tokyo, Setsubun ends with a spectacular sight. Hundreds of bronze lanterns hang from the broad eaves of Nara's eleven-hundred-year-old Kasuga Shrine. Thousands of lanterns, made of stone, stand in the gardens around the shrine and along the paths leading to it. On this evening, at a certain moment, all these lanterns are lit. This glowing welcome to spring is one of Japan's most beautiful sights.

Festivals of Spring, Summer, and Fall

As spring advances across the islands of Japan, various towns celebrate it in their own way. When the first plum blossoms appear at Kashima, on Tokyo Bay, the villagers choose a young boy to serve as what they call a child-godlike-person. Dressed in feudal armor, he is carried through the town on a farmer's shoulders. Costumed villagers follow. The man leading the procession blows deep notes on a big seashell, like the war horn feudal warriors once used.

Cherry trees begin to bloom late in March, in the warmer parts of Japan. By early April they are in bloom in cooler areas. For the next six weeks blooming trees may be seen, in one region or another, all over the country—on hillsides and in valleys, in public parks and private gardens, and around Buddhist temples and Shinto shrines. For all that time Japan is one vast moving festival celebrating the delicate pink bloom called *sakura*.

Because cherry blossoms fade within a few days, every Japanese has a special admiration for them. He feels that the briefness of their life adds a sadness to their beauty and makes them more precious than other flowers.

Japanese newspapers report where and when the best blooms may be seen. People often travel long distances to a famous cherry grove. Clubs hold noisy cherry-blossom dances. Families invite friends to a quiet sakura-viewing party. Together they sit in silent admiration of a single cherry tree.

September's full moon is honored with moon-viewing parties. The Japanese say this is the most beautiful moon of the year. People set up a tiny Shinto altar in their garden, or in some other quiet place. On it they place offerings of food, fruit, flowers, and grasses that ripen in autumn. Then, as they watch the silvery planet move across the sky, someone may read a poem about the moon or tell a moon legend. Everyone eats little moon-shaped dumplings made for this evening.

The shadows on the moon's surface are said to be particularly sharp on this night. The Japanese do not claim that these shadows form a human face, however. Instead of seeing a man in the moon, they see a rabbit using a mortar and pestle, a device for pounding grain into flour. Legend says the rabbit is pounding rice for the popular round cakes called *mochi*.

October festivals celebrate Japan's magnificent

chrysanthemums and maple trees. Chrysanthemums of the kind once grown only for the royal family, and hundreds of other varieties as well, now bloom in parks and in tubs along city streets for everyone to enjoy. When the maple trees, or *momiji*, turn crimson in the hills, there are momiji-viewing festivals today too, just as there have been in Japan for centuries.

Rice-Planting and Harvesting Festivals

Japan's most famous nature festivals celebrate the planting and harvesting of rice, the country's basic food. Although today Japanese often eat bread or potatoes in place of it, they still plant thousands of acres of rice each year. The success of each crop is vital to the whole country.

Farmers and their families perform rituals they believe will bring about a good harvest. Some of these rituals honor a much-loved deity called Jizo, said to be the guardian of children and departed souls. How Jizo also became the guardian deity of rice fields is told in an old legend.

One day, the legend says, a farmer fell sick before he finished planting his rice fields. After he recovered he saw, to his surprise, that the work had been completed. He could not learn who had done him this great favor, but he set off to a shrine to give thanks. On the way he passed a statue of Jizo and saw that the god's feet were muddy.

"It was Jizo who planted the rice!" he said. "That is how his feet became muddy!"

Today, in some villages, farmers make offerings of food and wine at Jizo's shrine. In other villages farmers throw handfuls of mud at each other, when the planting is done, or daub mud on a statue of Jizo. They are asking him to protect their fields.

One of the most famous rice-planting festivals takes place near the big industrial city of Osaka in June. It starts with a procession of *geisha*, or female entertainers, dressed as farm women.

First the procession goes to a shrine where the geisha pray for the crop and receive rice seedlings from the priest. Then, accompanied by farmers, musicians, and young men in ancient costumes, the geisha go to a special rice paddy inside the shrine enclosure. There they hand the seedlings to farm women who plant them.

Drums and flutes keep time with the planters as they bend down, over and over, each time pushing a seedling deep into the mud. The songs

the women sing, to ease their backbreaking labor, have been sung in Japanese rice fields for centuries.

The Star Festival—*Tanabata*

Early in July each year some Japanese cities and towns explode with color. Long bamboo poles have been set along the sidewalks in the business area. They are braced in such a way that they lean out over the streets. Fastened to these poles are thousands of paper chains, streamers, and pompons. They are yellow, green, blue, purple, red—every color of the rainbow.

At the same time branches of bamboo have been set around house doorways and in gardens. These are decorated with paper figures cut out by children.

This gay display celebrates Japan's romantic *Tanabata*, or Star Festival. It grew out of an ancient legend about the stars named Vega and Altair and was once a festival during which farmers prayed for good crops.

The legend says that Vega, daughter of a king of heaven and known as the Weaver Star, married Altair, the Cowherd Star. She was so happy as a bride that she neglected her weaving, and this made her father very angry. He banished Altair to the far side of the Heavenly River, or Milky Way, and decreed that the lovers could see each other only once a year. He said that Vega could meet Altair on the seventh day of the seventh moon.

When that day came, Vega could find no way to cross the river. She was weeping with disappointment when a flock of magpies took pity on her. They spread their wings to form a bridge, and Vega sped happily across it into Altair's waiting arms.

Ever since then, the legend says, when the sun shines on the seventh day of the seventh moon, the magpies form their bridge and the star lovers are reunited. But if it rains that day, the magpies cannot bridge the swollen river, and the stars must postpone their meeting for another year.

Once Tanabata was a simple country festival. Farmers made offerings of food to the Cowherd Star in the hope of a year of good farming. Their wives made offerings of cloth and asked the Weaver Star to help them become good weavers. Children offered romantic poems, written with great care. They hoped the star lovers would make them skillful in the art of writing with a brush and ink.

Now Tanabata has become a gay city carnival, especially for children and young people. Wandering up and down the colorful streets, they buy food and souvenirs at the many festival stalls.

But the paper decorations children make, to hang on the bamboo branches set up outside their homes, represent the offerings once made by farming families. On strips of paper they write poems with careful brush strokes. They cut paper into the shape of fruit and other foods. They fashion tiny paper kimonos.

This noisy city carnival also ends today as Tanabata always ended in quiet country villages. On the day after the festival, all the paper decorations and bamboo branches are taken down and thrown into a stream. The Japanese still believe that offerings carried away in this manner will bring them good luck.

6. The Year Ends, the Year Begins

New Year's Day, or *Genjitsu*, is such an important national festival in Japan that other smaller
festivals and fairs have grown up around it. This
celebration of the start of a new year, with all its
hopes and dreams for the future, thus spreads over
many weeks. It begins in November and stretches
into January.

Year-End Fairs

Special fairs take place in November at the
shrines honoring a trio of legendary princes. There
are several of these shrines in and around Tokyo,
and in other cities as well. The fairs are called

Cock Fairs because they occur on each Cock Day in the month. The twelve animal names given to years in the old lunar calendar are also used for the days of a twelve-day "week." So a Day of the Cock is the fifth day out of every twelve. There are always at least two of them in November. Sometimes there are three.

The stalls set up at Cock Fairs sell the New Year's decorations called *kumade*. These are bamboo rakes hung with tiny figures of gods of good fortune and other lucky symbols. They vary in size from a scant few inches to as much as several feet.

A man about to buy a kumade for his family usually likes an audience. He asks the price of the rake he has chosen and starts back in mock horror at the figure named. He offers to pay a quarter of that amount. The seller indignantly refuses and suggests a new price only slightly lower than his first. To the admiration of those around him, the buyer starts to walk away. Over his shoulder he offers perhaps a third of the original price. The seller counters with another reduction, and so it goes, offer and counteroffer, until the seller shouts a triumphant "Sold!" A man who pays less than half the price originally asked feels he has made a fortunate start toward a prosperous new year.

In mid-December, at a Battledore Fair, people buy the paddles used in battledore-and-shuttlecock. This is a traditional New Year's Day game for girls in Japan. It is similar to badminton, but it is played without nets. The players simply bat the "bird," or shuttlecock, back and forth with their paddles. Even girls who never play the game still want one of the latest model battledores to display during the holidays. These paddles were once decorated with delicate paintings. Now they usually carry pictures of beauty-contest winners or other popular figures of the day.

Late in December many people attend the Year-End Fairs which sell New Year's decorations for doors and gateways. Not everyone still uses these decorations. Even those who do may not know what they stand for. But ancient tradition says they express definite hopes and wishes for the coming year.

The *kado-matsu*, or gate pine, is a pine branch, a bamboo stalk, and a sprig of apricot or plum blossom. Each part of it has its own meaning. The evergreen pine symbolizes strength and a long life.

The bamboo symbolizes prosperity, uprightness, and constancy, because bamboo grows rapidly, stands straight, and bends in the wind without breaking. The apricot or plum blossoms, which often appear before the snow melts, are symbols of strength and nobility.

The other important traditional decoration, hung above the gate pine, is the rice-straw rope called a *shime-nawa*. It honors Amaterasu, the Sun Goddess, most important of all Shinto deities. Legend says Amaterasu was once so angered by her brother that she shut herself up in a cave, and thus left the world in darkness. The other gods begged her to leave the cave, but she ignored them. So they sang and danced and recited sacred texts until she grew curious enough to peek out. Then they held a mirror in front of her, and she was so delighted by her radiant image that she emerged.

To bar her return, and preserve light for the world, the other gods closed the cave entrance with a rope of rice straw. And ever since, the legend says, rice-straw rope has protected places from harm and evil.

Twisted into the rope used at New Year's are strips of white paper, a fern frond, a humpbacked lobster, and a bitter orange. The paper guards against the entrance of evil spirits. The fern's many tiny leaves express the hope that the family's wealth will multiply. The lobster (often an artificial one is used) represents the wish that all in the house will live until their backs are humped with age. The bitter orange, called *daidai*, symbolizes the continuity of family life, because daidai sounds like the word meaning "from generation to generation." This kind of pun, or play on words, is very common in Japan.

A special two-layered cake, often bought or made before New Year's, is called a mirror rice cake. It is an omen of good fortune because it represents the mirror Amaterasu looked into when she was lured out of the cave. The laurel leaves used to decorate it come from a bush that keeps its old leaves when the new ones appear. They stand for the unity of a family.

Today many people interrupt their New Year's preparations to celebrate Christmas. Less than one percent of the Japanese are Christians. But department stores have so successfully promoted the idea of Christmas gift exchange that non-Christians have adopted the custom.

Great Last Day

Finally the Great Last Day of the old year arrives. Businessmen try to pay all their debts and set their affairs in good order before the day ends. Then they hurry home through streets that have been decorated with green branches and paper streamers. Their wives have been busy cleaning, so their homes too are ready for the new year. Grown sons arrive with their own wives and children, to join their parents for this important evening. Everyone sits down together for a simple meal of *shoba.*

Shoba, usually bought ready-cooked from a shoba shop, are thin buckwheat noodles. They are longer than other kinds of noodles, and thus are said to symbolize long life. Children try to swallow at least one shoba whole, for luck. They let it slide down their throats, instead of chewing it.

Some families spend this evening at home, waiting to hear the deep-toned Buddhist temple bells that ring in the new year. The bells always toll 108 times. Buddhists say they are tolling away the 108 troubles or worldly cares that burden all living men. Other families visit a Shinto shrine, to pay their respects there at midnight, and to ask the help of the gods for the year to come.

Before returning home most shrine visitors buy good-luck charms from the stand just outside the shrine. One popular charm is a tiny figure of the new Animal of the Year. Young girls also buy folded slips of paper which tell their "fortunes." If a girl likes the one she has bought, she ties it to a tree or fence near the shrine. It is said this will make the good fortune come true.

New Year's Day

On New Year's morning all the members of a family dress in their best, often in new clothes bought for the holiday. Then they bow before their Buddhist altar and their Shinto shrine called a *kamigama*, or kami shelf. Usually this little shelf holds only a charm from some important shrine the family has visited. Then they sit down around a low table, or around the shallow pit which holds their cooking stove, and wish each other a happy new year.

The father pours spiced wine for everyone, beginning with the youngest. The mother serves bowls of the traditional New Year's soup, which contains vegetables and bits of rice paste or rice cake. She may also serve black beans, called *mame*,

whose name also means "strong," and a kind of seaweed that symbolizes happiness.

After breakfast the children receive their New Year's gifts, usually coins sealed in special gift envelopes. The New Year's cards arrive and are opened. Millions of holiday greeting cards are mailed in Japan each year, and postmen deliver as many as possible on New Year's morning.

If the weather is good, children spend much of the day outdoors. Boys fly kites. Girls play with their new battledores. Or their parents may take them to the nearest snowy slope for a family ski outing.

If the weather is cold and wet, boys and girls together may sit in a circle on the mat-covered floor and spread out the cards for an old New Year's game called Poem Cards. One player reads the beginning of a famous poem, and the others try to pick up the card bearing the poem's last words. Some Japanese know all these poems so well that they recognize each one from its first word.

New Year's is a family festival, with a great deal of visiting among friends and relatives. Everywhere there is plenty to eat and plenty of rice wine to drink. In the evening, however, many modern young

Japanese go off by themselves to a movie, a sports event, or a dance. They are more interested in modern fun than in the old traditions.

First Days

The celebration of a new year does not end with New Year's Day. January 2 is a holiday too. It is called *kakizome*, which means "first writing." The Japanese now write with ordinary pens and pencils. But many of them are so devoted to the ancient art of brush-and-ink writing that they form clubs and attend classes to improve their skill. This is the day they display that skill.

Every member of the family writes a poem or proverb on a long strip of paper. If one paper is particularly beautiful, it may be hung for a while in a small alcove called a *tokonoma*. This is where a Japanese family displays a single cherished possession and perhaps a blossoming branch or a few flowers.

Two days later, on January 4, most of the businesses and shops that have been closed since the Great Last Day open their doors again. Sellers of meat, fruit, and vegetables make their first deliveries of the year, in trucks festooned with banners.

On January 5 thousands of people go to an Ebisu. shrine, to buy good-luck charms. Plump smiling Ebisu, one of the seven Shinto deities of good fortune, has a special place in the hearts of all Japanese.

Another good-luck charm is sold at a special market festival held on January 6 or 7 in the small city of Takasaki, north of Tokyo. Called a *daruma*, it is a chubby doll without legs but with a weighted and rounded bottom. A daruma immediately rolls upright again, if it is pushed over. Thus it is said to symbolize an unconquerable spirit, a refusal to accept defeat.

The doll's painted eyes are often covered with paper, or it may have no eyes at all. Anyone who buys a daruma doll in January can therefore make a wish for the new year and uncover one eye or paint it in. Later in the year, if the wish comes true, he will give the doll its other eye as a reward.

January 7 brings an official end to the New Year's festivities. Street decorations are taken down, and children burn them in huge bonfires. Gate pines and shime-nawa ropes disappear.

At some time during the long holiday season, most people have made sure they fulfilled an ancient Japanese obligation: they have paid their respects to their superiors. Children have paid respects to parents and teachers. Workers have paid respects to employers. Grown-ups and children alike have paid respects to their ancestors and to their gods. Even in the midst of this gay festival, the Japanese have not forgotten their responsibilities.

But they have also enjoyed themselves as much as possible. And they look forward to enjoying the new year that lies ahead. Their calendars show that it too will provide them with many opportunities to dress in their best and go off to a festival.

PRONOUNCING GUIDE

chimaki	chi mah kee
dai	dah ee
daidai	dah ee dah ee
daruma	dah roo mah
futon	foo ton
geisha	geh ee shah
hi	hee
hibachi	hee bah chee
hina	hee nah
hoko	hoh koh
kado-matsu	kah doh mah tsoo
kakizome	kah kee zoh meh
kami	kah mee
kamigama	kah mee gah mah
kekko	keh koh
kumade	koo mah deh
mame	mah meh
matsuri	mah tsoo ree
mikoshi	mee koh shee
mochi	moh chee
sake	sah keh
sakura	sah koo rah
samurai	sah moo rah ee
shime-nawa	shee meh nah wah
shoba	shoh bah
shobu	shoh boo
shogun	shoh gun
tokonoma	toh koh noh mah
yama	yah mah
yabusame	yah boo sah meh

INDEX

95